I, WITNESS

VISION

My Story of Strength

Precious Perez

Norton Young Readers

An Imprint of W. W. Norton & Company
Independent Publishers Since 1923

Series edited by Anika Hussain, Zainab Nasrati,
Amanda Uhle, and Dave Eggers.

For information about permission to reproduce selections from this book, write to
Permissions, W. W. Norton & Company, Inc., 500 Fifth Avenue, New York, NY 10110

For information about special discounts for bulk purchases, please contact
W. W. Norton Special Sales at specialsales@wwnorton.com or 800-233-4830

Manufacturing by Lakeside Book Company
Book design by Hana Anouk Nakamura
Production manager: Delaney Adams

Library of Congress Control Number: 2024934151

ISBN 978-1-324-05387-3 pbk.

W. W. Norton & Company, Inc., 500 Fifth Avenue, New York, N.Y. 10110
www.wwnorton.com

W. W. Norton & Company Ltd., 15 Carlisle Street, London W1D 3BS

1 2 3 4 5 6 7 8 9 0

I would like to dedicate this book to all of my fans, friends, and family, who are all guiding lights in my life. It truly takes a village, and I wouldn't be where I am without each and every one of them. I'd like to dedicate this to all my professors and mentors who have guided me along my journey, and to the late Judy Heumann. I'd also like to dedicate this book to my hometown of Chelsea, Massachusetts, where I was born and raised, and to Puerto Rico, La Isla del Encanto. I dedicate this book to RAMPD (Recording Artists and Music Professionals with Disabilities), and to my bandmates in Midair Decision. Finally, this book is dedicated to all of my coworkers and to the young students of the Michael J. Perkins School in Boston and the Handel and Haydn Society, the Children's Academy Childcare and Preschool in Louisville, and all of my future students and coworkers, wherever they may be.

CONTENTS

CONTENTS

INTRODUCTION

Anika Hussain, Amanda Uhle, and Dave Eggers

One of the best ways to understand other people's struggles and achievements is to read their personal stories. That's what this series is all about: letting young people share their own experiences. Our hope is that by hearing one person's story, our readers will learn about others' obstacles and think of ways we might make the world more peaceful and equitable.

Teenagers like Malala Yousafzai and

Greta Thunberg became iconic for standing up for what they believe is right. Other teens, not yet as well known, have also stepped up to make a difference. When Adama Bah was a teenager in post-9/11 New York, she was falsely accused of being a terrorist simply because she is Muslim. She spoke up to defend herself and others like her. When Salvador Gómez-Colón was fifteen, his family endured Hurricane Maria in Puerto Rico. Using his deep local knowledge and incredible dedication to helping his neighbors, Salvador founded Light and Hope for Puerto Rico, raising money and gathering supplies to help islanders with basic needs during the emergency.

The I, Witness books bring you stories of young people like you who have faced extraordinary challenges in their lives. Their stories are exciting and surprising, filled with struggle—and humor and joy, too. We hope that you'll consider your own life and your own story as you read. Is there a problem in the world or in your life that you'd like to help solve?

In this book, you'll meet Precious Perez, who is from Chelsea, Massachusetts. She was born prematurely and health problems caused her blindness when she was an infant. Over and over, Precious and her mother heard from doctors and others about what she could not do. But Precious saw herself differently, and her mother fought for her right to be seen as a person, not just as a person with a disability.

As Precious grew, she experienced bullying and discrimination at times and always found solace in music. Whether it was her mother's Puerto Rican salsa music during housecleaning sessions or Precious's own sing-alongs to J. Lo CDs, music provided a safe haven throughout her younger years. Soon her teachers recognized that her love of music was paired with an enormous talent. Against the odds, Precious is making a successful career as a professional musician and music educator. She could have listened to the many voices over the years telling her what she could not do. Instead, Precious chose to focus on what she could do, which is incredible. Many of us will recognize the conflicts Precious has faced, and all of us will be moved by her strength and determination in the face of extreme challenges. As readers ourselves, we were heartened and inspired by Precious's story, and we hope you will be, too.

CHAPTER 1

Talent

It was a Monday morning during my senior year of high school. After four years, it seemed that I knew every corner at Chelsea High School and every person in it. The thirteen hundred students were multicultural and diverse. I was well known as the only blind person in the school, and

I found my classes mostly fun even though they were a little predictable.

But this day would be anything but predictable.

I was just setting my things down in my music production class when my teacher, Mr. Pappavaselio, asked me, "Precious, can I talk to you for a moment?"

Surprised, I immediately felt a sense of dread. *Am I in trouble for something? Have I missed a deadline or an assignment?* I thought.

Anxiously, I followed Mr. Pappavaselio across the small classroom and into one of the closets that had been converted to performance studios. He sat me down on a stool opposite him and, without any hesitation, asked, "Do you want to make an album, Precious?"

To say I was confused was an understatement, but he didn't seem to notice.

"I think you have a gift, and I know you write songs. I've seen what you can do in class, and I really think there's something we can do with your talent." He paused to emphasize his next words. "Because that's what it is: a talent."

The word *talent* bounced around in my brain a little. I wondered if I'd even heard him correctly. As far as I knew, albums were made by people like Jennifer Lopez and Mariah Carey. I was a public high school student in Massachusetts.

Mr. P was waiting patiently for me to answer—I hadn't spoken since he'd said "talent."

I smiled tentatively. "I mean, I have like a hundred songs, but . . ."

"If you're interested in making an album, I can help you." Mr. P's tone was earnest. "I *want* to help you. I have a friend who is a producer who could help develop the album and get the word out about your music. We could do a crowdfunding campaign to cover the costs. We could . . ."

He kept going on about how we could

record my music and release it to the public, but I was barely listening.

A few minutes earlier, I was beginning an ordinary school day. Now I was having a conversation about making my own album. I was in disbelief. Not because I thought I wasn't good. But at seventeen years old, for most of my life people had been telling me about the things I *could not* do rather than about the things that I *could*.

"You're serious?" I asked. "We could make an album?"

"Totally serious. I think we could make something great."

I was quiet again for a minute. I had to consider whether I could actually do this.

His suggestion was not only an endorsement of my talent but also his acknowledgment of my determination and my ability to pull off something as complex and important as this. I was honored.

As I sat on that stool across from my teacher, my doubts and anxiety evaporated. I've always been good at making decisions based on my own gut feelings. Two years earlier I'd attended the National Federation of the Blind's Massachusetts convention. It was my first time there and I learned so much about the inspiring activists working in my state for independence for blind people. When the then-president of the student division announced he would be leaving his position and they were having trouble filling the role, I stood up in the hotel conference room. "I'll do it," I said to a room full of strangers. I would go on to be the president of that group for seven years.

When an opportunity is right for me and allows me to grow and challenge myself, I jump in.

"Precious, what do you say?" Mr. P asked, the excitement in his voice clear.

"I'm in."

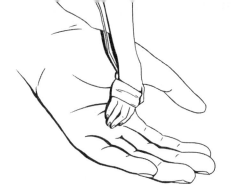

CHAPTER 2

Fighter

Blindness is all I know. Retinopathy of prematurity, or ROP, has been a part of my life for longer than I can remember.

I was born two and a half months early and the cards were stacked against me from that moment. I weighed only one pound when I was born. I was so small that my mom could hold me in one hand, her fingers able to close around my body. She dressed me in clothes meant for dolls from Toys "R" Us. They were the only things that would fit me properly. I looked so much more like a doll than a baby that my family often had to do double-takes just to make sure I was real.

But being small wasn't my only challenge. I had to be placed in an incubator for the first month of my life, my body unable to keep me warm. My skin was too thin, allowing my blood vessels to peek through, and my features appeared sharper and less rounded than a typical full-term baby's would.

During that time, I also had trouble breathing. I was given extra oxygen to assist my breathing, but that presented another problem. At some points, I was getting too much oxygen, which caused my retinas to detach. It's hard to imagine that oxygen could do so much damage, but premature babies are very fragile. My eyes had not developed fully before I was born, one of many risk factors for me.

With my retinas detached, I became blind. It didn't take long for doctors and others to begin telling my mom, grandma, and the rest of my family what I would not or could not do. It was like a conveyor belt, one after the other.

"She won't . . ." and "She can't . . ." to infinity.

"She won't be able to walk," one doctor said.

"She won't be able to talk," another doctor said.

"She won't be able to . . ."

"She'll never . . ."

"She isn't . . ."

It was always somebody telling my family what I wouldn't be able to do. And if they weren't telling them what was beyond my abilities, they were telling my family what distinct resources I would need. I'd need sensory play toys, or "special" places I would need to go, like a school for the blind.

"She won't be able to do things like other kids. It will be impossible."

The doctors may have been very knowledgeable and trying to help, but here's the thing they didn't know: My mom is a fighter. She always has been.

She was just fifteen when I was born and had navigated many challenges before then. There was no way she was going to stop fighting for what was right just because a doctor was telling her about all the things her daughter couldn't do.

In fact, she and my grandma found a doctor who believed in her and believed in me, too: Dr. Eduardo Budge at Mass General

Hospital in Chelsea. He, like my mom, saw me as much more than a blind person.

My mom was determined to raise me like any other child. She wasn't delusional. She knew, of course, that I'd face challenges others would not and that I'd need certain forms of support. But she rejected the idea that I should be set apart, that my every need should be accommodated. She had a vision for me to grow into an independent and fierce woman like her. She saw me as a person first and foremost, not *just* a disabled person. The distinction may seem minor. It's only a matter of a few letters, but it's one that makes a profound difference. That slight shift in perspective is what's shaped me into the person I am today.

But even though my mom knew that I was a person like anybody else, not everyone did.

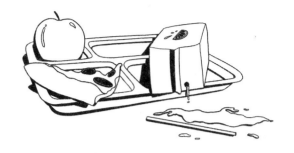

CHAPTER 3

Hurt

Even with my mom's stubbornness, I sometimes felt like an outsider during my childhood. In primary school things were somewhat easy. Kids that age mostly did not focus on my disability.

Middle school was a totally different story.

I've always loved school. It was the one place where, really, it didn't matter whether I was blind or not.

At the end of the day, with the right adjustments, I could still do my homework just like my peers. The language we used may have been different, but the result was always the same. Addition and subtraction in Braille were always going to yield the same output as written numbers would for my classmates. And the alphabet would still lead me from *A* to *Z* in the end. I needed certain materials to adapt, and I needed my teachers to describe to me clearly what was pictured on the board, but even so—I truly felt like anybody else. Doesn't every student need some help in school? That's why we're there, to learn. I never felt any different, because I was given reasonable accommodations.

But while academically nothing had changed between my peers and me, socially I felt like everything changed.

My classmates spread rumors about me and my mom.

"Her mom was drinking when she was pregnant with her and that's why she's blind," one girl said.

"You're a teacher's pet," another girl sneered.

"The world doesn't revolve around you," sniffed another.

They were saying so many unkind things about me, and all I could do was shut down. My anxiety skyrocketed from all the negative voices in my head day in and day out.

It wasn't just their words; it was their actions, too. In the middle school lunchroom, I'd sit down with my tray and out of nowhere someone would take it. I'd have to spend the rest of the time trying to find my food while everyone else was laughing at me.

Whether it was their jealousy or just kids being kids, I didn't care. At the time, all I felt was that there was something inherently wrong with me. I wouldn't be getting bullied if I wasn't blind.

And if I thought being bullied by my classmates was bad, the romance department was worse.

In my preteen years, I often spent time at my cousins' house on the weekends. Every weekend, I'd join my cousins and their best friend. The four of us would play outside and roam around the neighborhood. We usually walked to the Stop & Shop, and if I had the money I would buy a five-pound bag of Skittles, my favorite candy, to share.

One afternoon, my cousins' friend came over when I was at their place for a birthday party. For some reason I can't explain, it simply felt like we were meant to be. We clicked. The two of us were riding around on scooters, and it felt like we were straight out of a romantic comedy. We played games and talked as though we were already close enough to know just how the other person worked. He didn't treat me like the kids at school did. He didn't treat me like I was disabled.

So obviously I fell in love with him. It started with me just liking him as a person, and then it evolved into full-on infatuation. All the Taylor Swift songs in the world couldn't add up to how I felt about him. For his birthday, I made him a Braille birthday card. I even wrote a trilogy about our imagined love story and narrated an audiobook version.

I only saw him a handful of times, but every time I went to my cousins', I was desperately hoping that he would be there.

My fourteenth birthday party took place at my cousins' house, and like a miracle, the boy was there. I decided on that day that I was going to tell him how I felt. I would make him my boyfriend.

But before I could say anything, my aunt pulled me aside.

"Maybe you shouldn't tell him how you feel," she said.

"Why?"

"I overheard him talking."

"Okay?"

My aunt hesitated. Finally, she told me, "He said, 'How can she like me? She can't even see me.'"

"You're sure?" I asked. It was hard to believe he felt that way when he always seemed so happy to spend time with me.

"I'm sure," my aunt confirmed regrettably.

And that was all it took for our potential romance to end.

I thought he was treating me like a normal person, but I guessed I could never be normal in middle school. No matter what I did or said, people would always look at me differently.

I didn't want it to hurt. I'd been through

enough in school that it shouldn't have, but it hurt deeply.

I started to consider what it really meant to be attractive. Especially as I grew older and heard other people get compliments on their looks, I began to wonder: Why is appearance always part of why we like or don't like people?

I'd roam the hallways at school and overhear boys talking to girls, telling them how beautiful they were. I was never told that. I couldn't stop thinking about the complicated connection between body image and blindness.

According to what I was hearing, my worth would be dictated by how others evaluated my appearance. And how could I evaluate anyone without seeing them? I wanted my words to matter—my advocacy for people with disabilities, my ideas, all the things other than my appearance that make me, me.

CHAPTER 4

Voice

My entire life, I've been surrounded by music.

No one in my family was a musician, but everyone listened to music all the time. Saturday mornings, my mom dusted and mopped to salsa music, and we listened to reggae in the car on the way to the store.

The soundtrack to my life ranged from hip-hop and R&B all the way to jazz and classical, and, of course, Latin music. I used to spend hours singing along to songs on the radio, my audience consisting of the teddy bears in my bedroom. I was just too shy to sing in front of anyone, including my mom.

As I grew up, music became an untouchable safe space for me. It's my sacred escape. So, when my struggles started to feel like too much in middle school—the panic attacks, the ever-present bullying—music was a way out. Music allowed me to find my voice at a time when I didn't even know I had one.

When I was six, a family friend gave me

a Barbie karaoke machine. It was this bulky pink machine that came with a microphone and cassette tapes. I used to love pressing down on the chunky buttons, awaiting the whirring noise of the tape as it wound backward. I could sing along to the same songs over and over again.

Eventually I started using the echo effect, amplifying my otherwise soft voice, pretending I was onstage. I soon swapped out the microphone for a headset like the one pop stars used onstage and tried songs that weren't from the Barbie karaoke machine: Eminem, J. Lo, Mariah Carey, and others. When I sang in the comfort of my own home, I felt like nothing could hurt me.

I wasn't Precious who was blind or Precious who couldn't do this or that—I was just Precious. I could be who I wanted to be, no matter what anyone said.

A few months after I received the karaoke machine, I sang a musical pattern as part of a call-and-response during music class. My teacher paused for a moment when I finished.

"Precious, you have a really nice singing voice," she told me.

I wanted to hide, afraid that if anybody else overheard they would make fun of me. The attention felt uncomfortable.

But at the same time, I wanted her to say it louder. I wanted her to say it to everyone else in class and make them aware that I could do things. That I could be just as exceptional as my classmates. It was overwhelming to have someone outside of my immediate family recognize me for my singing. Before, I'd never dared to imagine that singing was something I could do outside of the walls of my bedroom.

With the newfound confidence my teacher inspired, I started singing more and more. The older I got, the more research I did into music production and various techniques for improving my sound.

"Listen to you, Precious, you sound just like Mariah Carey," my Uncle Pucho told me. Mom was driving, he was in the passenger seat, and I was lying down in the backseat of her car, humming along to the radio and then singing a bit. "You're singing like you're going to Berklee College of Music!"

I'd never thought about it before. Did people really go to college with the sole purpose of studying music? As much as I worked at music in my spare time, it didn't occur to me that I could do it as a profession. Singing was always a dream of mine, but at that point I didn't know if it was something I could do professionally. I mean, how could I pay my bills unless I somehow gained notoriety?

Being a professional musician had seemed like one of the many things on the growing list of things I couldn't do.

But the thought lingered in my mind, alternately seeming completely absurd and like the thing I most wanted in the world. Getting into Berklee was like getting into Harvard for musicians.

Improbable as it seemed, I realized I wanted to try. I wanted to keep singing. I wanted to grow into an artist, a songwriter, a singer. I wanted it all, and I was ready to work as hard as necessary to grow into a respected, professional musician.

CHAPTER 5

Album

Now that I knew what I wanted to work toward and that people could go to college to study music, Mr. P's offer to make an album seemed even more important than ever.

Mr. P and his producer friend, Doug Batchelder, worked together to take the songs I'd written and help me record and release them. On TV, making an album looks simple: you just see people singing while a guy behind a sound board mixes beats. But it's a lot more complicated than that.

Over the course of more than a dozen recording sessions, we crafted each section of every song, decided on arrangements, and recorded all the instruments. We listened to different versions to decide what we wanted to change or add, and tossed ideas back and forth. I had my longtime photographer friend Brian Snyder take photos of me for the album art. There was quite a bit to do beyond just singing in the studio.

After the album was finally recorded and produced, I was itching to get it out to listeners. However, it's not as easy as just uploading it to Spotify and asking them to arrange all the bits behind the scenes. You've got to set up a website, create physical copies of the album, think of a marketing strategy to sell it to the fans, sign up with a performing rights organization to register your music, partner with a distributor to release it to digital stores, and so much more.

To pay for this project, Mr. P suggested we use Kickstarter. A crowdfunding campaign is basically a way for people around the world to contribute to a project with the click of a button. It's also a way for people like me to make their creative dreams a reality.

At the time, I wasn't deeply connected in the music industry. Working with a platform like Kickstarter allowed me to raise the money we needed for the album while also beginning to build a fan base, a group of people invested in my work. They'd all take a meaningful, if small, role in the album. Their money would help fund my music, and in turn it would be like a piece of them would be in my songs. I thought it was a beautiful process, and it reminded me of how music made me feel when I was younger—how I could feel connected to the artists through their music, wishing they knew just how much I appreciated them. Through the Kickstarter, my fans would be able to do just that.

So, in addition to all the behind-the-scenes work to produce the album, we also built a fundraising plan, grew a community of supporters online, and continually updated all the backers on our progress.

Mr. P helped me put together the Kickstarter—a blurb for the page and regular updates to the backers. He also helped me with the page layout and with spreading it across social media.

Even with his great help, it was tough to imagine hitting my goal of $2,500. It was especially stressful because if you don't hit your financial goal by your deadline, you don't get to keep any of the money raised. I didn't know many people who had the ability to throw money at a project like this. Unless somebody knew me, it would be difficult for them to find my project. As the days ticked by, I began to feel that raising funds this way was really a long shot. I started to lose faith that we could do it.

Things turned around when I was invited to speak at the Environmental Travel Companions fundraising event. The Environmental Travel Companions are dedicated to making outdoor adventures more accessible for people with disabilities and those who are under-resourced. They believe that opportunities to spend time in nature are part of building everyone's self-confidence and well-being. I'd worked with them a couple of times in the past, and during my Kickstarter campaign they invited me to attend the gala as their speaker.

When I arrived, the executive director, Diane, was kind enough to pull me aside and chat with me.

"I've listened to your music online, Precious, it's wonderful," she said.

I thanked her and tried not to squirm at the compliment. "I'm trying to release an album with the help of a teacher. We have a Kickstarter online to help fund it."

She asked how it was going.

"There's not long left and we're not anywhere near our goal, to be honest." I gave a tight-lipped smile, not wanting to put a downer on the evening. I had to admit that the Kickstarter always loomed in the back of my mind, and I was very worried it would not succeed.

"Well," she said, choosing her words carefully, "I can't advertise your campaign here at the gala, since we're already fundraising for the Environmental Travel Companions, but I can spread the word to my friends and other colleagues in case they are able to donate anything."

At this point, with only thirty days left, I was happy for any type of advertisement. If we didn't make the goal for the Kickstarter, all that money people had pledged would be lost to us, and all our efforts would have been wasted.

"What's your goal?" she asked.

"Two thousand five hundred."

"Okay, I'll spread the word after the gala."

And she did. I watched her that evening chatting with people and introducing me to different investors who might be interested in my story and my music.

I appreciated her efforts. Still, I couldn't help but fear that, just like the doctors had said when I was born, this was just another thing I wouldn't be able to actually do.

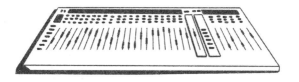

CHAPTER 6

Countdown

The first few days after the gala, it seemed like I might in fact reach my goal. With help from Diane, money started trickling into the Kickstarter and we were soon halfway there. We were receiving donations and building up a fan base at the same time, which was incredibly exciting. Mr. P and I worked even harder on spreading the word on social media. I spent more hours than I can count sharing snippets of my songs to build interest, and I told just about anybody who would listen about the campaign. I was suddenly the opposite of shy about myself and my musical abilities.

But with three days left, we were still missing about one thousand dollars.

I couldn't bear to think about what would happen if we didn't make the goal. Not only would I be disappointed, but so would those who had generously pledged and helped me so much along the way. If I didn't reach my goal, I truly felt it would be like giving up. I thought of all the doctors who told my mom,

"She'll never . . ." and "She can't . . ." I was not going to let them win.

I could feel my confidence withering. Even though I knew in the back of my mind that my worth didn't depend on whether we got the money for the album, I still felt very unsure in those final hours. I decided that, money or not, album or not, I would always be an artist. I had the performances and recordings to prove it.

But having that album out there for the world to see. . . . I wanted to feel validated.

I took a moment for myself, closing my laptop and stepping away from the stress of the Kickstarter campaign. I turned on a song I loved that I could cry and sing to. I hooked up my microphone and allowed the music in my headphones to surround me like the coziest blanket on a cold December evening. With the microphone in my hand, I could forget for just a little while how much was at stake.

I tried to ignore the ticking clock and focus on my singing. If I didn't take good care of myself, who would?

Now, with two days left and about one thousand dollars to go, I'd mostly given up hope.

Then I opened my laptop back up, refreshed the Kickstarter page, and saw I was no longer under my goal, but over it. A woman named Vivian had made a major gift, and we shot past the goal.

I couldn't believe it.

We had exceeded our goal.

I was going to be making an album.

But most of all, I couldn't stop thinking about how I had finally proved everyone wrong.

I *could* do things that others deemed impossible.

And, in fact, I could do them better.

I poured my thoughts and my gratitude into an email to Vivian. I hardly knew what to say beyond a heartfelt, "Thank you." She wrote back promptly.

"You know, Precious, many people in this world with 20/20 vision are 'blind'! Ironic as it may sound, it is true. You see with your soul and heart. You see with your feelings and emotions. My dear Precious, I wish you the best of life and happiness."

CHAPTER 7

Berklee

With the album now guaranteed to be out in the world, I had ticked off one of my goals, but I still had another to check off: going to college to study music.

Berklee College of Music was one of those music schools that everybody talks about, on par with Harvard or Yale. It was *the* school for music, and it seemed like going there—or not—spoke volumes about one's musical abilities.

I hadn't wanted to be part of that narrative. I was confident enough to understand that I could probably make it in, but I didn't want to apply. I didn't want to conform. I wanted to break out of what I'd known and my hometown. I wanted independence.

My friends and family encouraged me to at least give it a try. It was effectively right in my backyard, about five miles from my home. They asked, "What's the worst that could happen if you apply?" If I applied and I got in, I could always turn it down if it wasn't for me.

I gave in and applied. The audition and interview processes were like those of any other music school, with questions about why I thought Berklee was a good fit for me. For the audition, I sang two contrasting pieces, a classical piece and a contemporary cover of Alicia Keys's "If I Ain't Got You." I hadn't gotten much sleep the previous night but thought I did okay on both elements.

A month later, I got an acceptance letter.

The only problem? My financial aid package didn't cover the $60,000 annual tuition and fees. There was no way I could take out multiple loans. The repayment process seemed completely overwhelming, and my family is low-income. There was no way we could afford this cost without additional scholarship support.

I'd finally decided that Berklee was indeed for me, and now it was falling out of reach. I tried to convince myself that I was better off going somewhere else.

But my teacher of the visually impaired—Janet Ulwick-Sacca—pushed me to write an appeal letter.

"It's not going to hurt you to appeal the decision," she said. "The worst that can happen is that they won't provide any additional funding, which is the situation you're in now."

She was right, of course. I'd been back and forth so many times on my college decision that none of this seemed to matter much anymore.

My titiLisa helped me write the appeal letter. We pulled every heartstring we could, pleading for financial help. We sprinkled in every possible bit of woe. We lamented how heartbreaking it was that the only thing stopping me from achieving my dreams was my family's financial situation.

While I was awaiting a reply to my plea to Berklee, I received a full-ride scholarship to a Christian college. My only qualm was that it was a liberal arts college rather than a dedicated school for music. This meant that on top of my music specialization, I would have had to complete classes outside of my major, like theology or finance—which wasn't what I wanted. I wanted to study music and music only. I'm a Christian, but I didn't plan on studying religion. It felt like an impossible choice. Even though this situation was not ideal, it was the only financially viable option I had. What else could I do?

My heart wasn't in it but I urged myself to commit to the Christian college. It was probably what I needed, and what my family and community needed. There was no way

I could justify going into debt for the rest of my life.

The day before my deadline to make a final decision, I received a phone call.

Someone from Berklee's appeals office informed me they were going to award me an additional $20,000. This generous amount still wasn't enough to cover all of my tuition, but with the scholarships and minimal loans, along with a projected increase in scholarships over time, it meant that attending Berklee would be possible. Difficult, but possible.

I couldn't believe it.

I had twenty-four hours to decide. It should have been obvious; I should have chosen Berklee without a doubt. Yet, after many weeks of convincing myself that I ought to go to the other school because of finances, I struggled to sort it out.

I called on all of my people that night, asking their thoughts and mulling over the pros and cons of each school repeatedly. Later that night, unable to sleep, I finally rolled out of bed. I opened my laptop and got out my credit card. On the Berklee website, I scrolled to "make a tuition deposit," clicked, paid, and crawled back under the covers.

The next morning I announced on Facebook that I was going to Berklee. I knew deep in my heart that I wouldn't be happy had I gone to the other school. It was a fully classical music program, and I wanted to be versatile, encompassing Latin music and pop and R&B and all the genres I'd always loved. It was also an enclosed campus and nowhere near Boston or my family.

Berklee was right for me.

That's not to say it was easy. At Chelsea High School, I was one of two people known for their voice. But at Berklee? I was one of six thousand talented musicians. I was a small fish in a giant pond when all I'd known my entire life was the feeling of standing apart from others, either because of my voice or because of my disability. Walking among all these brilliant people, I didn't feel like I mattered much, and that was an important test for me. I had to come to terms with my humility. Once again I was fighting and working twice as hard because I carried with me certain labels. Low-income. Woman. Person of color. Person with a Disability. Working on making a name for myself in a place where everybody else was doing the same was a huge and challenging adjustment.

Eventually I realized that I was at Berklee for a reason. The panel wouldn't have accepted me had they not seen something special in me. They wouldn't have increased my financial aid package if they didn't think I had potential. They knew, just as I was remembering, that I had something to contribute not only to the school but to the music industry. I was unique and I was blessed, and I had to remind myself of that throughout my entire time at Berklee. I couldn't be anything but myself, and I could use my intersecting identities to advocate for myself and my communities. I found myself at Berklee, which wasn't something I thought I could do.

Rejection is hard. I experienced so much of it, from discrimination to various school music competitions. All of it hurt.

"I don't know how to teach you, since you're, you know, blind," one professor said.

"We've never had a blind student in this major before. We don't have accommodations in place," another professor said.

It wasn't just that I was a small fish in a big pond. I was not the first blind student at Berklee, but I was the first blind student to go through the music education major at the institution. I had to prove myself every second of every day. There was simply no room for me to mess up or not know something. I had to be on point at all times.

It was hard, but I knew I had to do it. For me. For my family. For my community. For anyone following my path. For everything that I'd worked toward my entire life. I felt this was God's purpose for me.

I wanted to shatter barriers and make the voiceless heard. I found a way to be resilient at Berklee because I knew it was a rare chance to use my position and help those who would come after me.

But even with all those barriers and the rejection I faced, I found my people. I was able to lean on Professor Chi Gook Kim in the assistive technology lab, the first blind professor at Berklee; he taught me all I know about music technology from the blindness perspective, as well as how to build what eventually became my artist website. I was able to rely on individuals in various departments who stood in my corner as I navigated everything from financial aid paperwork to scheduling issues. I cherished my friends, fellow Blind Berklee musicians, with whom I could commiserate about accommodation issues and other aspects within the disability experience that others couldn't quite fathom. I also learned immeasurably from professors and mentors who understood me and saw me for who I am, from rehearsal buddies to bandmates and Berklee cafeteria staff. My success would not have been possible without them. I learned so much about myself as a musician and a person, and gained more family and friends while studying abroad in Valencia, Spain.

In 2020, I learned that long ago Berklee had a Disability Club, but it had been dormant for many years for lack of participation. So many of us did not have a space to reflect and strategize together and to support one another. I gathered the club again, with Professor Kim as our adviser. We met weekly and all students with disabilities were welcome—whether they faced cognitive, physical, or developmental disabilities. Allies were welcome, too. While supporting one another was our main goal, we also were able to work together to bring our concerns and plans to Berklee administration as a collective. It benefited us all.

In my final year, I helped identify a successor—a drummer on the autism spectrum who was ready to take over

Disability Club leadership from me and help continue this important resource for future generations of Berklee students.

I built a community around myself because it was the only way to move forward. Berklee was what I made it, and I found my way of making it work for me as the artist I knew I was and the person I was becoming.

CHAPTER 8

Labels

Blindness might be all that I know and it might have defined me in the eyes of society for longer than I can remember, but in spite of all of that, I am so much more.

I first began to understand myself as an activist in 2021. A blind activist rapper recommended I join a new group in October of that year. Soon I was a member of the Recording Artists and Music Professionals with Disabilities (RAMPD), a global network of professionals with disabilities working to promote inclusion, elevate disability culture, and advocate for accessibility within the music industry. Founded by award-winning artists Lachi and Gaelynn Lee, RAMPD partners with the Recording Academy, the group that bestows Grammy Awards. RAMPD worked with the organizers of the sixty-fourth Grammy Awards to create a visible stage ramp, sign language interpretation on the red carpet, and live captioning and audio description for the event. I became more and more active in this group in my first year of membership, and as of September 2022, I'm its vice president.

I am a songwriter and a musician. I am an educator and a mentor. My husband and I formed a band, and we are performers. I am a graduate of Berklee College of Music. I am fiercely Boricua. I am low-income. I have anxiety and depression. I am a disability advocate. I am an author. I am a changemaker. And, among my other intersecting identities, I am also blind.

What I've learned along my journey is that people will try to put you in boxes with certain labels, and when they've put you in a box, they will tell you what you can or cannot do. Here's the thing: A box has eight vertices, ten edges, and six faces—and each side can have a label that defines the box. So, while people have gone to great lengths to define me as one thing, I am living proof that one thing is never enough. I am the sum of all my labels—there are many different parts of myself that, when combined, make me who I am. You can't have a song without the melody, rhythm, and lyrics coming together in perfect harmony.

When I introduce myself, I'm proud to go through all of my labels. People will often stick to the first one they hear about me without remembering that we are all multifaceted.

When those doctors told my mom about all the things I *couldn't* do, they didn't take into consideration all the things that I *could* do. They didn't recognize that I could fluctuate between my disability and being Hispanic and low-income and even a successful artist. They tried to put me into one kind of box.

I work hard not just for me but also for my communities. If I can be open about all the labels that identify me, I hope I can show others that they, too, can identify and express themselves with multiple labels.

Be stubborn, and don't listen when people tell you about what you can or can't do. Only you know what you are capable of. If you don't believe in yourself, nobody else will.

Find your people. Discrimination is real, and people won't always take time to understand your point of view, but there's help along the way. I've achieved what I have not just by myself but with the help of those around me. If it weren't for my mom standing up for me or my teachers encouraging me to sing, who knows where I would be today?

My blindness isn't what solely drives me, but it is a big part of what motivates me. My experiences with my disability are what allow me to see the world the way I do.

My music largely reflects what I've been

through. I use music as a vehicle for change and as an opportunity to uplift every aspect of myself and those around me. It's a way to share my experiences with the world so that more people can understand what it's like to be me: someone who doesn't fit neatly into one kind of box.

Because boxes aren't meant to be closed up. They're meant to be opened.

Continue the Discussion

What is ROP?

ROP, or retinopathy of prematurity, is an eye disease that affects many premature babies (born before thirty-seven weeks of pregnancy). ROP occurs when the retinas, the nerve tissue that lines the back of the eye, are not fully developed. The result may be bleeding in the eye or scarring that results in retinal detachment as the scar tissue pulls the retina away from the back of the eye, resulting in vision problems.

What is Braille?

For those who cannot use sight or are blind, Braille is a system for reading and writing specific language through touch. Braille can be coded into nearly every language and can be used all over the world. In addition to promoting intellectual freedom, equal opportunity, and personal security, Braille is a vital literacy tool for blind and visually impaired individuals.

What is Precious doing now?

In December 2021, Precious graduated with a double major in music education and vocal performance from Berklee College of Music. She got married to Shane Lowe, a percussionist, audio engineer, concert nerd, and music director, in August 2022. They played a concert with their band, Midair Decision, that same night in their wedding regalia. She was recently elected as vice president of Recording Artists and Music Professionals with Disabilities (RAMPD), a global network with the mission to elevate disability culture, promote inclusion, and advocate for accessibility within the music industry. She is also a member of the Recording Academy. Precious now lives in Louisville, Kentucky, where she is an Arts for All Kentucky teaching artist providing music enrichment for preschoolers at Children's Academy. She is focusing on her artistry with the goal of becoming the first blind Latina artist at the forefront of the music industry.

Where can Precious's music be heard?

Precious's music can be streamed on major platforms such as YouTube, Apple Music, Facebook, and Spotify.

What are some of the challenges students with visual impairments face in school?

Not having access to Braille is a major obstacle. Blind students often use Braille to navigate classroom numbers, assignment submission boxes, and other resources. Textbooks and other reading materials are often only available in written form. This makes blind students reliant on help from teachers or peers.

Social barriers are also common. Many people often feel they are responsible for guiding a visually impaired person—that is not the case. Although there may be difficulties and the person may have trouble getting to certain places, they are perfectly capable of looking after themselves. One of the biggest challenges, however, is the feeling of constantly having to prove oneself as capable. Even when that feeling might be unnecessary, that pressure exists for many and is very complicated to navigate.

Get Involved

1. Empathize.

Open your mind and your heart. Everyone is different from you, and you are different from everyone else in your own way. Don't let this make you afraid to approach someone.

2. Learn.

Do your research, and ask questions. It's always better to ask politely than to be left not knowing, especially when it comes to disability.

3. Share positivity.

Spread love and light everywhere you go, in every way you can. Always try to be as inclusive and unifying as possible. Just as music brings people together, so should we all strive to do just the same.

Engagement guide available. Find out more at wwnorton.com/i-witness-series

Timeline

1749

Denis Diderot publishes the essay "A Letter on the Blind, for the Benefit of Those Who See," highlighting that blind people are able to live satisfying lives and emphasizing the role of the sensory experience in human accomplishment, further developing the idea that sight is not central to the ability to understand and reason. The essay also foreshadowed the nineteenth century invention of Braille.

1829

Louis Braille invents the raised-point alphabet, but the method doesn't become well known or recognized until thirty years later.

1860

Braille is taught for the first time in the United States at the Missouri School for the Blind.

1940

The National Federation of the Blind is founded by Jacobus tenBroek, who was blind from the age of fourteen, along with Dr. Newel Perry. The Federation acknowledges that being visually impaired does not define a person or a future and reminds people that the visually impaired can live the lives they want without being held back.

1945

Berklee College of Music is founded.

1965

The first National Federation of the Blind scholarships are awarded.

1990

The Americans with Disabilities Act (ADA) is passed by Congress, establishing one of the most comprehensive pieces of civil rights legislation in American history. This year marks the fiftieth anniversary of the National Federation of the Blind.

1995

The National Federation of the Blind establishes a technology through dial-up synthetic speech that makes the daily newspaper available to the visually impaired by six-thirty a.m. on the day of issue.

1998

Precious is born two and a half months premature.

2004

Precious receives the Barbie karaoke machine that changes everything.

2010

Journal of Blindness Innovation and Research, published by the National Federation of the Blind's Jernigan Institute, becomes the world's first professional journal that addresses blindness's real challenges from the perspective of blind people, their parents, and their teachers.

2016

Precious records and produces her debut album.

2022

Precious graduates from Berklee College of Music.

Author's Acknowledgments

Special thanks to Pete Pappavaselio and Doug Batchelder for being instrumental in helping me kick-start my music career and just for being amazing musicians, people, and dear friends. Special thanks to Lachi for lifting me up and supporting and advising me in everything I do. Thank you to my incredible husband Shane Lowe, unmatched musician in his own right and my everything. Thank you to my mom, Jennifer Alvarez, for making me the woman I am today, and to all of my siblings, family, and friends. And to my village, in which I am blessed to say there are too many to name, but they know who they are. I carry all of you with me in my heart and mind every day, in all that I do. Whether through actions big or small, you have made such an enormous impact on me, and I vow to make you proud and lift you up every chance I get.

Editors' Acknowledgments

The editors would like to extend special thanks to the Young Editors Project (YEP), which connects young readers to manuscripts in progress. The program gives meaningful opportunities for young people to be part of the professional publishing process and gives authors and publishers meaningful insights into their work. Early readers of this manuscript include Corinne Licardo of New York City; Daniel Grain of Donegal, Ireland; Ruby Mae Harker of South Yorkshire, UK; Zahra Almosawi, Juanee Draper, Jaslynn Hayden, Isabella Jimenez, Amari Martin, Greidis Martinez,

Areej Mousa, Baramsha Musa, CJ, Scarlette Pitts, Abigayle Richardson, Layla Grace, Montserrat Rodriguez, Madina Aliyevam, La'Chaiya Arthur (Kai), JaeLynne Berry, Keirstyn Brown, Karen Byrd, Briseyda, Alessandra M., Lailah Nguyen, and Na'Shyia Whiteside of Young Authors Greenhouse in Louisville, Kentucky; Suzanna, Simón, Caleb, Amayah, Jackie, Aimee, Jacob, Jaxon, Chloe H., Malechi, Gus, James, Haven, Adri, Brady, Sam, Luke, Chloe G., Amelia, Gianna, Ella, Dylan A., Mason, Clara, Rockii, Brooklyn, Jay, Amaea, Emily, Lucas, Naomi, Jesse, Penny, Henry, Paige, Daniela, Alandria, Eli, Allie, and Maddox of Ashley Morse's classroom in Albuquerque,

New Mexico; Eli Daly, Maia Reyeros, Jaxson Valentine, Taran Jordan, Landen Miller, Ava Ingersoll, Holden Heuberger, Dylan Oliver, Sophia Weisgerber, Brooke Vey, Parker Deklotz, Pearl Klune, Nalani Resa, Levi Conlan, Henry Mills, Naul Renteria Rangel, and Graysen Hearing of Dawn Green's classroom in Carnation, Washington; Skanda, Peyton, Miles, Kenneth, Joanna, Jensen, Jacob, Eddie, Finlay, Evan, Elizabeth, Eli, Dylan, Mariem, Thomas, Rui, Layla, Eddie, Reyana, Austin, Alexis, Alex, Zane, Yara, Malcolm, and Landon of Meadowlands Public School in Ontario, Canada.

Special additional thanks to Kristin

Allard, Simon Boughton, Nyuol Lueth Tong, Zoë Ruiz, Claire Astrow, and Hannah Rose Neuhauser.

www.youngeditorsproject.org

About I, Witness

I, Witness is a nonfiction book series that tells important stories of real young people who have faced and conquered extraordinary contemporary challenges. There's no better way for young readers to learn about the world's issues and upheavals than through the eyes of young people who have lived through these times.

Proceeds from this book series support the work of the International Alliance of Youth Writing Centers and its sixty-plus member organizations. These nonprofit writing centers are joined in a common belief that young people need places where they can write and be heard, where they can have their voices celebrated and amplified.

www.youthwriting.org